Deliver Your Soul From Evil

Johannes Tefo

Published by Johannes Tefo, 2023.

Also by Johannes Tefo

Family spiritual Warfare Books
Youth's Guide To Spiritual Warfare
A Women's Guide To Spiritual Warfare

Standalone
Deliver Your Soul From Evil
Overcoming Spirit Of Stagnation
The 24: Prophetic Word For This Season 2024 And Beyond
Michael For Warfare
Territorial Spirits: Overcome Evil Strongholds in Your Life And
Take Over Your Community With Strategic Warfare And Winning Prayers
Prayers Against Suicide Spirit
Spiritual Warfare When Enough is Enough
Identity In Christ
Prayers Against Satanic Networks
The Workplace You Need: Spiritual Warfare Prayers That Silence Evil Powers At Your Workplace.

Table of Contents

I dedicate this my friends and family in Christ. Be free in the name of the Lord. Blessed is He who comes in the name of the Lord.

1. **Prayer:** Prayer is a powerful tool that Christians can use to connect with God and ask for His protection and guidance. Through prayer, believers can ask for strength to resist temptation and for the courage to stand up to the devil.

2. **The Word of God:** Reading and studying the Bible can help Christians gain a deeper understanding of God's teachings and develop a stronger spiritual foundation. The Bible can provide guidance on how to resist temptation and overcome spiritual challenges.

3. **Fasting:** Fasting involves abstaining from food or other pleasures for a period of time as a way to focus on spiritual growth. Christians may use fasting as a way to strengthen their faith and resist temptation.

4. **Fellowship:** Connecting with other believers through worship, prayer, and other activities can provide Christians with support and encouragement. Fellowship can also help Christians stay accountable to their spiritual goals and provide a sense of community.

5. **Forgiveness:** Forgiving others and seeking forgiveness for one's own mistakes can be a powerful way to overcome negative influences and strengthen one's spiritual connection with God.

6. **Worship:** Worshiping God through music, prayer, and other activities can help Christians focus on their spiritual connection with God and resist negative influences.

7. **Love:** Showing love and compassion to others, even in the face of adversity, can be a powerful way to resist

negative influences and strengthen one's faith.

UNSEEN REALM

The unseen realm is more real than you think. I am glad these days Christians and non-believers all over the world are awakening to the unseen realm. Revelatory knowledge is unveiled before our own eyes like never before. With all that said, I am not implying that the devil is anywhere near or equal to God. But you can feel, sense, and see his presence, which will at times be the opposite of what God does.

With so many spiritual revelations, technology, and science at rocket heights, the enemy is also at the door to offer something that feels godly while it is not. From inception, the enemy has long been rival with the human race trying to substitute the government of God in our lives with his own kingdom that looks appeasing but deadlier than a cobra's venom.

The aim of this personality called, Satan, is to kill, steal, and destroy. To divert the call of God and dilute the fire within our hearts with evil sensations. But glory to God since many around the world are waking up from their sleep of death which is spiritual ignorance. Ignorance of the holy spirit in our lives will cost us a lot. The saving grace of the Living God is limited when there is a high level of ignorance of the voice of God.

Isaiah 55 says harken unto my words you shall live and eat. Prosperity and success comes from being sensible to the voice of God and doing what He tells you to do. You can name them, healing, deliverance, miracles, and so on, they all manifest through the word of God. Harkening to the voice of the Living God increases our faith for us to be bold like lions and release words that translate to tangible things in the physical world. This beautiful world of ours is built upon faith. It was by faith that Elohim spoke this world into existence. Remember that you are walking on a spiritual earth, found by spiritual principles of God—called faith.

When we are engaging in spiritual warfare, the weapons we use are spiritual weapons. Apostle Paul wrote for us a perfect and holy spirit-inspired hierarchy of the dominion of the kingdom of darkness—powers and thrones in high places, rulers of spiritual darkness of this world, and principalities in heavenly places. I grew up with phony teaching that says the devil lives in hell.

From the spiritual encounters I have had throughout my walk with God, I can without a doubt tell that the devil has dominion or kingdom in hell but does not live in hell. He has three dominions; the high places in the heavenly, the marine kingdom on earth, and hades or hell in the underworld. These three kingdoms' mission is to deceive, manipulate, and control the inhabitants of the earth, people, animals, and world system.

His main mission is to turn this world into satanic worship assisted by other fallen angels, demons, and human agents who sold their souls to the dark science of the kingdom of darkness. Though, he is not all-powerful since he is not omniscient like God. He can only be at one spot at a time. This is one of his weaknesses. The kingdom is strengthened by its unity, its hierarchy structure, and many people around the nations following this worldly system in their mentality, deeds, and actions opposing the Holy Spirit.

The truth of God is what shall set the people of this world free. Christ is that covenant to the nations of the earth to purge us with his precious holy blood.

2 Chronicles 7:14 If my people, which are called by my name, shall humble themselves, and pray, and seek my face, and turn from their wicked ways; then will I hear from heaven, and will forgive their sin, and will heal their land.

This is the secret to warfare. When this scripture says *"Shall humble themselves"* here it talks about prayer and fasting. By the way, fasting is an act of humility before the presence of God. Prayer will always be on top of the list as a weapon of warfare and deliverance. There is basically nothing you can do without a life of prayer. Not only prayer but strategic and serious prayers that put you on the spot in every kingdom. The kingdom of God backs up warriors in Christ. The same applies, the kingdom of the enemy seeks after the souls of prayer warriors to steal, kill, and destroy.

Battlefield of warfare

This battle did not start in the garden of Eden. It started in heaven where archangel Michael was ordered to cast down Lucifer from heaven. Actually, he was Lucifer before he became Satan—the deceiver. The world Satan describes his motive and action. In our modern day, we can call it a job description.

Isaiah 14 and Ezekiel 28 give a detailed description of his fall. The root of his fall was pride and rebellion—and iniquity was found in him. He was no longer fit to be before the presence of God through his dealings. Dealings can refer to connection, transitions, or business. Any man who has had an encounter with this dark prince had to bargain with him. Look how our mainstream celebrities are not even ashamed to flash out their ties with this personality called the Devil. Even worse, our so-called men of God and women of God are also following the same route.

I had deep revelations about men and women of God who sold their souls to the dark side for fame, power, and money. Some will go around looking for power to demonstrate miracles, healing, and deliverance in their church. For the most part, it is all deception. As someone who was unknowingly initiated into occultism in church, I can without a doubt attest that many pastors, prophets, apostles, and bishops serve the god of mammoth(money). The church is just a way of raising funds for their lavish lifestyles.

Every individual must study the bible to show themselves approved. This is a set time for the move of God and the enemy knows it. The enemy is unleashing dark forces like never before to limit us from reaching the spiritual height God wants us to be. The spirit of religion is blinding many with dark blinders to never see the truth. We must allow the holy spirit to eliminate all the religious cultural traditions of man-made doctrines. The battle is on.

The battlefield of spiritual warfare is a place where the forces of light and darkness clash in a great and eternal struggle. For we wrestle not against flesh and blood, but against principalities, against powers, against the rulers of the darkness of this world, against spiritual wickedness in high places.

In this great battle, we must put on the whole armor of God, so that we may be able to stand against the wiles of the devil. We must gird our loins with truth, and put on the breastplate of righteousness. We must take the shield of faith, wherewith we shall be able to quench all the fiery darts of the wicked. And we must take the helmet of salvation, and the sword of the Spirit, which is the word of God.

For we know that the weapons of our warfare are not carnal, but mighty through God to the pulling down of strongholds. We know that we have not been given a spirit of fear, but of power, and of love, and of a sound mind. And we know that if God be for us, who can be against us?

Therefore, let us be strong in the Lord, and in the power of his might. Let us fight the good fight of faith, and lay hold on eternal life. Let us be steadfast, unmovable, always abounding in the work of the Lord. And let us not be weary in well doing, for in due season we shall reap if we faint not.

For the Lord is our refuge and our strength, a very present help in times of trouble. He is our shield and our buckler, our high tower and our fortress. He is the God of our salvation, in whom we trust. And he has promised that he will never leave us nor forsake us.

Therefore, let us go forth into the battlefield of spiritual warfare, knowing that we are not alone, but that the Lord is with us. Let us fight with all our might, and let us never give up the fight, for the victory is already won, and the crown of glory awaits those who are faithful unto the end.

Preparing war

As a follower of Christ, you are engaged in a spiritual battle that requires constant vigilance and preparation. The enemy is real, and he seeks to steal, kill, and destroy (John 10:10). However, do not be discouraged or afraid, for you have been given the power and authority to overcome the enemy (Luke 10:19).

To prepare for spiritual warfare, there are several things that you can do. Firstly, you need to know who you are in Christ. You are a child of God, redeemed by the blood of Jesus, and empowered by the Holy Spirit. You are loved, valued, and chosen by God (John 1:12, 1 Peter 2:9). Therefore, you must resist the lies of the enemy and hold onto the truth of God's Word.

Secondly, you need to put on the armor of God (Ephesians 6:10-18). The armor consists of the belt of truth, the breastplate of righteousness, the shoes of peace, the shield of faith, the helmet of salvation, and the sword of the Spirit, which is the Word of God. Each piece of armor represents a spiritual truth that you must apply in your life. For example, the belt of truth represents the need to know and live by the truth of God's Word.

Thirdly, you need to be in constant prayer and fellowship with God. Prayer is a powerful weapon in spiritual warfare (Ephesians 6:18). Through prayer, you can ask for protection, guidance, and strength. You can also intercede for others and pray against the schemes of the enemy. Additionally, regular fellowship with God through Bible reading, worship, and fellowship with other believers, strengthens your faith and helps you discern the voice of God.

Fourthly, you need to live a life of obedience and holiness. The enemy often uses sin and disobedience to gain a foothold in our lives. Therefore, it is important to repent of sin and strive for holiness. This means living a life that is pleasing to God and aligns with His Word. It also means avoiding things that are contrary to God's will and purpose for your life.

Finally, you need to stay alert and be prepared for spiritual attacks. The enemy does not give up easily and will often come at us when we least expect it. Therefore, it is important to be vigilant and watchful. When you sense an attack, pray for protection, and use the armor of God to defend yourself.

In conclusion, preparing for spiritual warfare requires a daily commitment to knowing God, putting on the armor of God, praying, living a life of obedience and holiness, and staying alert. Remember that you are not alone in this battle, for the Lord is with you (Isaiah 41:10). Stand firm in your faith, and trust in the Lord's power and protection.

May God bless you and keep you strong in the battle.

As we live our lives as followers of Christ, we must be aware that we are engaged in a spiritual battle. The enemy is not something to be taken lightly, for he is real and seeks to steal, kill, and destroy (John 10:10). However, do not be discouraged or afraid, for you have been given the power and authority to overcome the enemy (Luke 10:19).

To prepare for spiritual warfare, we must start by understanding who we are in Christ. We are children of God, redeemed by the blood of Jesus, and empowered by the Holy Spirit. We are loved, valued, and chosen by God (John 1:12, 1 Peter 2:9). Knowing our identity in Christ is crucial because it enables us to resist the lies of the enemy and hold onto the truth of God's Word.

Once we know our identity in Christ, we must put on the armor of God (Ephesians 6:10-18). The armor of God is not a physical armor, but a spiritual one. Each piece of armor represents a spiritual truth that we must apply in our lives. For example, the belt of truth represents the need to know and live by the truth of God's Word. The breastplate of righteousness represents the need to live a righteous life, while the shoes of peace represent the need to be ready to share the gospel. The shield of faith represents our faith in God's promises, while the helmet of salvation represents the assurance of our salvation. Finally, the sword of the Spirit represents the Word of God, which is our weapon in spiritual warfare.

In addition to putting on the armor of God, we must be in constant prayer and fellowship with God. Prayer is a powerful weapon in spiritual warfare (Ephesians 6:18). Through prayer, we can ask for protection, blessings, and other things.

Chapter 1: The Power of Prayer

Prayer is one of the most powerful spiritual weapons available to us. It is a way to connect with God and communicate with Him directly. Through prayer, we can seek guidance, ask for forgiveness, and find strength to overcome life's challenges.

Prayer is not just a one-way conversation; it is a two-way dialogue between the believer and God. Christians can pray for themselves and for others and can ask for specific things or simply seek God's presence and peace. The Bible is full of examples of prayer, from the Lord's Prayer to the prayers of David and other biblical figures.

One of the most important aspects of prayer is faith. God hears and responds to prayers according to His will. This requires trust in God's wisdom and love, even when it is difficult to understand His plan.

Prayer can take many forms, from traditional prayers recited in church to spontaneous prayers spoken in the moment. Declarations, decrees, and proclamations are some of the powerful spoken prayers that take a prophetic form. Some Christians find it helpful to set aside specific times each day for prayer, while others prefer to pray whenever they feel the need.

In addition to individual prayer, you can also pray in groups, whether in church services or small prayer groups. This kind of communal prayer can provide support and encouragement to believers and can help build a sense of community and sense of belonging during spiritual warfare.

There are many different kinds of prayer, including intercessory prayer, which is when you pray on behalf of others, and contemplative prayer, which involves quiet reflection and listening for God's voice. You can also use prayer to express gratitude, confess their sins, and seek wisdom and guidance.

Prayer is not a magic formula for getting what one wants; rather, it is a way to deepen one's relationship with God and align oneself with His will. Without a doubt, we believe that prayer can bring comfort, strength, and peace, even in the midst of life's difficulties.

Prayer is a powerful spiritual weapon that can help Christians overcome temptation and find strength in God. It is a way to connect with God and seek His guidance and can provide comfort and support in times of need. By making prayer a regular part of their lives, Christians can deepen their relationship with God and experience the transformative power of prayer.

Prayer as warfare arsenal

One of the most powerful weapons that Christians have in their arsenal when it comes to spiritual warfare. Through prayer, believers can connect with God, tap into His wisdom and strength, and receive His protection and guidance in the midst of the battle.

When it comes to defeating the enemy, prayer is essential. The Bible tells us to "pray in the Spirit on all occasions with all kinds of prayers and requests. With this in mind, be alert and always keep on praying for all the Lord's people" (Ephesians 6:18, NIV). This means that we should be praying not only for ourselves but also for other believers who are facing spiritual battles.

One of the ways in which prayer is effective in defeating the enemy is by giving us access to God's power. As we pray, we invite God to work in our lives and in the lives of those we are praying for. God's power is greater than any force of darkness, and through prayer, we can tap into that power and overcome the enemy.

Prayer also helps us to stay focused on God and His purposes for our lives. When we pray, we are reminded of God's love for us and His plan for our lives. We are able to align ourselves with His will and His purposes, which helps us to resist the enemy's attacks and overcome his schemes.

Another way in which prayer is powerful is by providing us with a sense of peace and calm in the midst of the storm. When we face spiritual battles, it can be easy to become overwhelmed and anxious. However, when we pray, we are reminded that God is with us and that He is in control. This gives us a sense of peace that helps us to stay strong and focused on the battle at hand.

In order to make the most of the power of prayer, believers should cultivate a regular habit of prayer. This includes setting aside time each day to pray, as well as praying throughout the day as needs arise. It is also helpful to pray with other believers, as there is strength in numbers and corporate prayer can be particularly effective in defeating the enemy.

In conclusion, prayer is an essential tool for believers when it comes to spiritual warfare. Through prayer, we can access God's power, stay focused on His purposes, and experience a sense of peace and calm in the midst of the battle. By cultivating a regular habit of prayer and praying with other believers, we can effectively defeat the enemy and live a victorious Christian life.

Chapter 2: The Importance of Scripture

Scripture, or the Bible, is the foundation of Christian faith. It is a collection of books that were written over the course of many centuries by various authors, all of whom were inspired by God. The Bible is the authoritative and trustworthy source of God's teachings and can provide guidance for daily life.

One of the main reasons that Scripture is so important to us is that it provides a way to understand God's character and will. The Bible contains stories of God's interactions with humanity, and through these stories, we can learn about God's love, mercy, and justice.

Scripture can also help us to understand our own identity and purpose. The Bible teaches that humans were created in God's image and that each person has a unique role to play in God's plan. By studying Scripture, Christians can gain insight into their own talents and gifts and can discern how best to use them for God's glory.

Another important aspect of Scripture is its ability to provide comfort and guidance in times of difficulty—especially during trial seasons. The Bible contains many stories of people who faced adversity and overcame it with God's help. These stories can provide hope and encouragement to believers who are struggling with their own challenges.

In addition to its spiritual benefits, Scripture also has practical value. The word is the sword of the spirit that dismantles the evil plans of the devil in our lives, family, and society. Engaging scriptures in faith will in no time amount to serious results in our lives. For we a fighting with the unseen realm which requires faith more than anything else. Thanks to God for opening our spiritual eyes through His spiritual gifts.

There are many different ways to engage with Scripture. Some Christians prefer to read the Bible from cover to cover, while others focus on specific books or passages. Some read Scripture on their own, while others participate in group Bible studies or attend church services where the Bible is discussed.

Regardless of the approach, I believe that Scriptures are living dynamic texts that can speak to us in different ways at different times. We believe that through the Holy Spirit, Scripture can guide us in our daily lives, providing wisdom, comfort, and direction.

In conclusion, Scripture is a vital component of Christian faith. It provides a way to understand God's character and will, helps Christians to understand their own identity and purpose, and provides comfort and guidance in times of difficulty. By engaging with Scripture on a regular basis, Christians can deepen their relationship with God and experience the transformative power of His word.

Importance of scriptures in warfare.

The importance of Scripture in spiritual warfare cannot be overstated. The Bible is not only the foundation of our faith, but it is also a powerful weapon in the battle against the enemy. Scripture is a source of truth, guidance, and wisdom that we can use to overcome the enemy's attacks and live a victorious Christian life.

One of the most powerful aspects of Scripture is its ability to expose the enemy's lies and deception. Satan is known as the father of lies, and he uses deceit to lead people astray from God's truth. However, Scripture is the ultimate truth, and it exposes the enemy's lies and deception for what they are. When we read and meditate on Scripture, we are equipped with the truth that we need to resist the enemy's attacks and live in victory.

Scripture is also a source of strength and encouragement for believers in the midst of spiritual battles. The Bible is filled with stories of people who faced trials and tribulations, and yet remained faithful to God. These stories serve as examples for us to follow when we face our own battles. Scripture reminds us that God is with us, and that He will never leave us or forsake us.

In addition, Scripture provides us with the tools we need to fight the enemy. The apostle Paul wrote, "For the word of God is alive and active. Sharper than any double-edged sword, it penetrates even to dividing soul and spirit, joints and marrow; it judges the thoughts and attitudes of the heart" (Hebrews 4:12, NIV). Scripture is a powerful weapon that we can use to discern the enemy's tactics and to counter his attacks.

To make the most of the power of Scripture in spiritual warfare, believers should cultivate a regular habit of reading and meditating on the Bible. This includes not only reading Scripture, but also studying it, memorizing it, and applying it to our lives. It is also helpful to pray over Scripture, asking God to reveal His truth to us and to help us apply it in our lives.

In conclusion, the importance of Scripture in spiritual warfare cannot be overstated. Scripture is a source of truth, strength, and encouragement that we can use to overcome the enemy's attacks and live a victorious Christian life. By cultivating a regular habit of reading and meditating on Scripture, we can effectively fight the enemy and experience the fullness of God's blessings in our lives.

Chapter 3: The Role of Community in Christian Faith

Community is an essential part of the Christian faith. We as Christians are not meant to live in isolation but to be part of a larger body of believers who can support, encourage, and challenge one another. Through community, we can deepen our relationship with God and grow in our faith.

One of the main benefits of community is the opportunity for fellowship. When we gather together, whether in church services, small groups, or other settings, we are able to experience a sense of belonging and connection with others who share their beliefs. This sense of belonging can be especially important for those who are feeling lonely or isolated.

Community also provides a way for Christians to learn from one another. In the community, people can share their experiences, insights, and struggles, and can learn from the wisdom of others. This kind of mutual learning can help individuals to deepen their understanding of God's teachings and to grow in their faith.

In addition to fellowship and learning, the community can also provide accountability. That we are accountable to one another for our actions and attitudes. This kind of accountability can help individuals to stay on track with their faith and to avoid falling into destructive patterns of behavior.

The community can also provide opportunities for service and outreach. We are called to serve others and to share the love of Christ with the world. Through community, as individuals, we can find ways to serve our neighbors and to make a positive difference in their communities.

Finally, a community can be a source of support and comfort in times of difficulty. When individuals face challenges such as illness, job loss, or family problems, the support of a caring community can be invaluable. Christians believe that they are called to bear one another's burdens and to offer practical and emotional support to those who are struggling.

In conclusion, community is an essential part of the Christian faith. Through fellowship, learning, accountability, service, and support, community can help individuals to deepen their relationship with God and to grow in their faith. By participating in community, Christians can experience the transformative power of God's love and grace.

Community of Believers during warfare.

Community plays an essential role in the Christian life, especially during times of spiritual warfare. In the Bible, we are called to live in community and to support and encourage one another. The apostle Paul wrote, "Therefore encourage one another and build each other up, just as in fact you are doing" (1 Thessalonians 5:11, NIV).

When we are facing spiritual battles, we need the support of our brothers and sisters in Christ. We need people who will pray for us, encourage us, and hold us accountable. In a community of believers, we can find strength and comfort in knowing that we are not alone in our struggles. We can also learn from the experiences of others and gain insight into how to navigate our own battles.

In addition to providing support and encouragement, community can also help us stay grounded in our faith. During times of spiritual warfare, it can be easy to become discouraged or distracted by the enemy's attacks. However, when we are surrounded by other believers who are also seeking to live out their faith, we are reminded of the truth of God's word and encouraged to remain steadfast in our beliefs.

Community can also help us grow in our relationship with God. Through fellowship with other believers, we can learn more about who God is and how He works in our lives. We can also share our own experiences of God's faithfulness and be inspired by the experiences of others.

To make the most of the role of community in spiritual warfare, it is important to be intentional about our relationships with other believers. This includes being open and vulnerable with one another, praying for and encouraging one another, and holding one another accountable in our walk with Christ. It also means being active in our local church and seeking out opportunities to connect with other believers.

In conclusion, community plays a vital role in the Christian life, especially during times of spiritual warfare. By seeking the support and encouragement of other believers, we can find strength and comfort in the midst of our struggles. We can also grow in our relationship with God and be encouraged to remain steadfast in our faith.

Chapter 4: Prayer and Its Importance in Christian Life

Prayer is a fundamental part of Christian life. It is a way for believers to communicate with God, to express their thoughts and feelings, and to seek guidance, comfort, and strength. Christians believe that prayer is a powerful tool that can help them to deepen their relationship with God and to experience His presence in their daily lives.

One of the main benefits of prayer is that it provides a way for Christians to express their gratitude to God. Christians believe that everything they have, including their very existence, is a gift from God. Prayer provides a way for them to acknowledge God's goodness and to thank Him for His blessings.

Prayer can also be a way for Christians to ask for forgiveness. Christians believe that they are all sinners and in need of God's forgiveness. Through prayer, they can confess their sins and ask for God's mercy and grace.

In addition to gratitude and confession, prayer can also be a way for Christians to seek guidance and direction. Christians believe that God is a loving and wise Father who wants to guide them in their lives. Through prayer, they can seek God's will and ask for His guidance in making decisions.

Prayer can also be a way for Christians to seek comfort and strength in times of difficulty. When facing challenges such as illness, loss, or fear, prayer can provide a sense of peace and hope. Christians believe that God is with them in all circumstances and that He can provide the strength and courage they need to persevere.

Another benefit of prayer is that it can help Christians to cultivate a deeper relationship with God. Prayer is a way for believers to spend time with God, to listen to His voice, and to experience His presence. Through prayer, Christians can grow in their understanding of God's character and will, and can deepen their love for Him.

There are many different ways to pray, and Christians can choose the methods that work best for them. Some prefer to pray alone, while others enjoy praying with others in groups or in church services. Some use written prayers or traditional prayers, while others prefer to speak spontaneously from their hearts.

Prayer is a vital part of Christian life. Through prayer, believers can express their gratitude, confess their sins, seek guidance and direction, find comfort and strength, and deepen their relationship with God. Christians believe that prayer is a powerful tool that can help them to experience the transformative power of God's love and grace.

Prayer is a powerful weapon in spiritual warfare, and it is essential for believers who want to defeat the enemy. In the Bible, we are encouraged to pray at all times and to pray without ceasing (1 Thessalonians 5:17). Prayer allows us to communicate with God, seek His guidance, and ask for His protection.

When we face spiritual battles, prayer is our first line of defence. It allows us to bring our concerns, fears, and struggles before God and seek His intervention. Through prayer, we can ask for God's wisdom and discernment as we navigate difficult situations. We can also ask for His protection and for Him to send His angels to watch over us.

Prayer is not just a one-way conversation. It is also an opportunity for us to listen to God's voice and discern His will. As we spend time in prayer, we can develop a deeper relationship with God and gain a greater understanding of His character and His ways.

One of the benefits of prayer is that it strengthens our faith. When we see God answer our prayers and work on our behalf, it builds our confidence in Him and in His ability to protect us. This faith can help us to stand firm in the face of opposition and to trust that God is with us, no matter what.

Another benefit of prayer is that it helps us to stay focused on God's truth. When we pray, we can ask God to remind us of His promises and to help us to meditate on His word. This can help us to combat the lies and deception of the enemy and to stay grounded in the truth of God's word.

In assumption, prayer is an essential tool for believers who want to overcome the enemy in spiritual warfare. It allows us to communicate with God, seek His guidance, and ask for His protection. Prayer also strengthens our faith, helps us to stay focused on God's truth, and builds a deeper relationship with Him. As we make prayer a regular part of our lives, we can experience the power and the benefits of this important spiritual weapon.

Chapter 5: The Importance of Bible Study in Christian Life

I always stress the power of bible study as it eliminate man-made ideology about the gospel of Christ. The truth can only set men free. The truth cries through the scriptures. The Bible is the central text of our faith. It is the inspired Word of God, and it provides the foundation for our beliefs and practices. Bible study is an essential part of Christian life, as it provides a way for believers to deepen their understanding of God's teachings and to grow in their faith.

One of the main benefits of Bible study is that it provides a way for Christians to learn about God's character and will. The Bible contains stories of God's interactions with humanity, as well as teachings on morality, ethics, and spirituality. Through Bible study, Christians can gain insights into God's nature, His plans for the world, and His expectations for believers.

Bible study can also be a way for Christians to develop their own spiritual practices. The Bible contains many examples of prayer, meditation, and worship, as well as teachings on how to live a God-centered life. Through Bible study, we can learn about the different spiritual practices and can incorporate them into their own lives to defeat the enemy and life the best life Christ died for.

In addition to learning about God's teachings and spiritual practices, Bible study can also provide a way for Christians to deepen their relationship with God. It is a living text, and God speaks through His words. Through Bible study, Christians can experience a sense of connection with God, and can feel His presence and guidance in their lives.

Bible study can also be a way for Christians to connect with other believers. Many churches and Christian organizations offer Bible study groups or classes, where believers can come together to study and discuss the Bible. Through these groups, Christians can share their insights, ask questions, and learn from one another.

There are many different ways to study the Bible, and Christians can choose the methods that work best for them. Some prefer to read through the Bible systematically, while others prefer to focus on specific books or themes. Some use study guides or commentaries, while others prefer to read the Bible and draw their own conclusions.

In conclusion, Bible study is a vital part of Christian life. Through Bible study, Christians can learn about God's teachings and spiritual practices, deepen their relationship with God, and connect with other believers. Christians believe that the Bible is the inspired Word of God, and that studying it can help them to grow in their faith and live a more God-centered life.

Chapter 6: The Power of Worship in Christian Life

Worship is an integral part of Christian life. It is a way for believers to express their love and gratitude to God, to honor Him, and to experience His presence in their lives. Worship is a powerful tool that can transform their hearts and minds, and can help them to live a more God-centered life.

One of the main benefits of worship is that it provides a way for us to connect with God on a deeper level. Worship can involve singing, praying, meditating, and reflecting on God's word. Through these activities, we can focus our minds and hearts on God, and can experience a sense of awe and reverence for His power and love.

We cannot talk about worship and not talk about David. David changed the way we praise, worship and sing to the Lord. We sing out our hearts and rent them out for the kingdom of the Living God if we are to experience the power of worship. Paul and Silas broke the bands of wickedness—chains fell through the power of worship. Worship brings the glory down. God bows down the heavens and hear us when we wear the garment of praise. It eliminates all the nasty feelings of worry, anxiety, stress and depression. I will urge you to worship in spirit and truth.

Worship can also be a way for us to express our emotions and feelings to God. God created us with emotions, and that He desires for us to express them to Him. Through worship, we can express their joys, sorrows, fears, and hopes to God, and can experience a sense of peace and comfort.

In addition to providing a way to connect with God and express emotions, worship can also be a way for Christians to cultivate a sense of community with other believers. Worship often takes place in a communal setting, such as a church service or prayer meeting. Through these gatherings, Christians can share in the experience of worship with others, and can support and encourage one another in their faith.

Another benefit of worship is that it can help us to focus on what is truly important in life. In today's fast-paced world, it can be easy to become distracted by worldly concerns and priorities. Worship provides a way for us to step back from the distractions of daily life and to focus on God and His kingdom.

There are many different ways to worship, and we can choose the methods that work best for them. Some prefer to worship in a more formal setting, such as a church service, while others prefer to worship in a more informal setting, such as in nature or in their own homes. Some prefer to worship through music and singing, while others prefer to worship through prayer and meditation.

In conclusion, worship is a powerful tool in Christian life. Through worship, believers can connect with God, express their emotions and feelings, cultivate a sense of community with other believers, and focus on what is truly important in life. Christians believe that worship is a vital part of their faith, and that it can help them to grow in their relationship with God and live a more God-centered life.

Worship as the warfare weapon

Worship is a powerful weapon in spiritual warfare, and it plays a crucial role in the life of a believer. In the Bible, we see that worship is a central theme throughout the Old and New Testaments. It is a way for us to express our love and adoration for God, to connect with Him on a deeper level, and to invite His presence into our lives.

One of the key ways in which worship is powerful in spiritual warfare is that it shifts our focus from our problems to God. When we worship, we are declaring that God is bigger than any obstacle or challenge we may be facing. We are reminding ourselves that He is in control and that He is faithful to keep His promises. This shift in focus can help us to gain perspective and to approach our battles with a renewed sense of hope and confidence.

Worship also has the power to break through spiritual strongholds. In the Bible, we see that when the Israelites worshipped, the walls of Jericho came tumbling down (Joshua 6:20). Similarly, when we worship, we are inviting the presence of God into our lives, and His power has the ability to break through the strongholds of the enemy. This can include addictions, unhealthy patterns of thought, and other areas in which we may be struggling.

Another benefit of worship is that it creates an atmosphere of peace and joy. When we worship, we are focusing on the goodness of God and on the truth of His word. This can help to calm our minds and our hearts, and to bring us a sense of peace even in the midst of difficult circumstances. Additionally, worship has the power to lift our spirits and to fill us with joy, which can be a powerful weapon against the enemy's attacks of discouragement and despair.

In conclusion, worship is a powerful weapon in spiritual warfare. It helps us to shift our focus from our problems to God, to break through spiritual strongholds, and to create an atmosphere of peace and joy. As we make worship a regular part of our lives, we can experience the power and the benefits of this important spiritual discipline.

Chapter 7: Fellowship in the lenses of warfare

———

I am always fascinating when I read the book of Daniel and how Daniel and his three friends we able to be victorious in a wicked Babylonian world. Besides individual prayers, these brothers supported each other spiritually. Comforting and praying for each other's family. And above all, they had the common ideal love for Jerusalem.

Looking at the example of Daniel and his three friends, we can see how important fellowship is for those who seek to live a life of faith and devotion to the Lord God.

In the face of great adversity and opposition, Daniel and his friends were able to stand firm in their faith, and this was due in large part to the strength and support that they received from each other.

Their fellowship was a source of encouragement, comfort, and accountability, and it helped them to remain faithful to the Lord God in a foreign land and a hostile culture.

In the same way, fellowship is essential for us as believers today. We need the support and encouragement of our brothers and sisters in Christ, to help us remain faithful and to grow in our walk with the Lord.

Through fellowship, we are able to share our struggles and triumphs, to offer support and encouragement, and to hold each other accountable to the standards of righteousness and holiness that are set forth in God's word.

Furthermore, fellowship allows us to use our gifts and talents for the benefit of the body of Christ, to serve and minister to one another, and to be a witness to the world of the love and power of the Lord God.

In all these ways, fellowship is a vital component of the Christian life, and it is essential for our spiritual growth and well-being. Just as Daniel and his friends were strengthened and encouraged by their fellowship, so too can we be strengthened and encouraged by the fellowship of believers, as we journey together towards our ultimate goal of eternal life in Christ Jesus.

Fellowshipping with other believers is an essential tool in the arsenal of every Christian. It allows believers to come together, share their experiences, encourage one another, and strengthen their faith in God. This is particularly important when facing spiritual battles, as it is through fellowship that believers can effectively defeat the devil.

The devil's primary tactic is to isolate believers and make them feel alone in their struggles. He tries to convince believers that they are the only ones facing their particular challenges and that they are powerless against him. However, when believers come together in fellowship, they realize that they are not alone in their struggles. They can draw strength from one another and share strategies for overcoming the devil's attacks.

Fellowship also provides believers with a platform to pray and intercede for one another. Through prayer, believers can ask for God's intervention and protection against the devil's schemes. They can also pray for one another's spiritual growth and protection, knowing that their prayers are more powerful when they are united in purpose.

Moreover, fellowship helps believers to stay accountable and to avoid falling into the devil's traps. When believers share their struggles and hold each other accountable, they are less likely to give in to temptation and sin. They can also encourage one another to keep their eyes fixed on Jesus, the author, and finisher of their faith.

In conclusion, fellowshipping with other believers is a potent weapon in defeating the devil. It provides believers with strength, encouragement, accountability, and a platform for prayer and intercession. Therefore, it is important for believers to prioritize fellowship and to seek out opportunities to connect with other believers regularly.

Fellowshipping with other believers can take many forms, including attending church services, participating in small group Bible studies, or joining prayer groups. It is through these interactions that believers can build meaningful relationships with other Christians, sharing their joys, struggles, and testimonies.

Church services offer believers the opportunity to come together in worship and receive instruction from God's word. This can be a time for believers to hear from God and gain insight into how to live a life pleasing to Him. Additionally, church services can provide a sense of community and belonging as believers gather together to worship and learn.

Small group Bible studies provide a more intimate setting for believers to share their experiences and to gain understanding from one another. These groups can focus on specific topics or Bible passages, providing a chance for believers to dive deeper into God's word and apply it to their lives. Through these studies, believers can receive encouragement and support from one another as they face common challenges and struggles.

Prayer groups are another avenue for fellowship, allowing believers to come together and lift one another up in prayer. These groups can be focused on specific needs, such as praying for healing, deliverance, or spiritual growth. When believers pray together, they are reminded of God's power and faithfulness, and their faith is strengthened.

In addition to the spiritual benefits of fellowship, there are also practical benefits. For example, when believers face financial or material needs, other believers can come alongside them and provide support. This could be through giving financial assistance, providing food or clothing, or simply offering a listening ear and words of encouragement.

In conclusion, fellowshipping with other believers is essential for defeating the devil. It provides believers with strength, encouragement, accountability, and a platform for prayer and intercession. Moreover, it offers practical support in times of need. As believers come together, they can overcome the devil's attacks and live a life that honors God.

Power of Daniel Fast

The story of Daniel and his three friends is a powerful example of the role that fasting can play in the life of a believer, especially when it comes to spiritual warfare.

As we know, Daniel and his friends were taken captive by the Babylonians and were brought to the king's palace, where they were to be trained in the ways of the Chaldeans. But from the very beginning, they made a decision to remain faithful to the Lord God of Israel.

One of the ways they did this was through fasting. When they were offered meat and wine that had been offered to Babylonian gods, they refused and asked for vegetables and water instead. They did this not only to obey God's law but also to abstain from the defilement that came from eating food offered to idols.

Through their decision to fast, Daniel and his friends were able to remain pure and focused on the Lord. Their bodies were strengthened and their spirits were sharpened, allowing them to be fully engaged in the spiritual battle that they faced.

Later on, when Daniel was praying and seeking the Lord, he again fasted and humbled himself before God. In doing so, he was given a vision that helped him to understand the spiritual warfare that was taking place behind the scenes.

This shows us that fasting is not just about abstaining from food or drink; it is about humbling ourselves before God and seeking His will and His ways above our own. Fasting helps us to tune out the distractions of the world and to focus our minds and hearts on the Lord, allowing us to discern the spiritual battles that are taking place all around us.

Furthermore, fasting is a powerful weapon in the arsenal of the believer when it comes to spiritual warfare. As we fast and pray, we are strengthened in the Lord and empowered by His Spirit. We become more sensitive to His leading and are better able to resist the schemes of the enemy.

In conclusion, the story of Daniel and his three friends teaches us the power of fasting in the life of a believer, particularly when it comes to spiritual warfare. Through fasting, we can remain pure and focused on the Lord, discern the battles that are taking place in the spiritual realm, and be empowered by the Holy Spirit to resist the enemy's attacks.

Faith is power

Faith is a powerful force that has the ability to transform lives, overcome obstacles, and bring about great things. It is the belief in something that is beyond our physical senses, beyond what we can see or touch, and it is the foundation of our relationship with God.

Faith is not just a passive belief or intellectual agreement with certain ideas; it is an active trust and dependence on God, a confidence in His character and His promises. It is the assurance of things hoped for, the conviction of things not seen (Hebrews 11:1).

Throughout history, there have been many examples of people who have demonstrated incredible faith in the face of great adversity. Abraham, for example, was called to leave his homeland and journey to a new land that God had promised him, without knowing where he was going. But he trusted God and went, and God blessed him abundantly.

Moses had faith that God would deliver his people from slavery in Egypt, and he led them through the Red Sea to freedom. David had faith that God would give him victory over Goliath, and he defeated the giant with a single stone.

In the New Testament, we see examples of people who had faith in Jesus and were healed, such as the woman with the issue of blood and the centurion's servant. And we see the faith of the early church, who were willing to suffer persecution and even death for the sake of the Gospel.

But faith is not just for the heroes of the Bible or for those who lived in the past. It is for us today as well. We are called to live by faith, to trust God and His promises, and to walk in obedience to His will.

Faith is not always easy, and there are times when it is tested and stretched to the breaking point. But it is in those moments that our faith can grow and deepen, as we learn to rely more fully on God and His grace.

In conclusion, faith is an essential component of the Christian life. It is the foundation of our relationship with God, the assurance of things hoped for, and the conviction of things not seen. Through faith, we can overcome obstacles, accomplish great things, and live a life that is pleasing to God.

Faith during spiritual warfare

Faith is an essential element in spiritual warfare. When we face spiritual battles, we must rely on our faith in God to overcome the enemy's attacks.

The Bible tells us that our battle is not against flesh and blood but against the rulers, against the authorities, against the powers of this dark world and against the spiritual forces of evil in the heavenly realms (Ephesians 6:12). This means that we cannot fight this battle on our own strength or our own understanding, but we need to rely on God's power and wisdom.

Faith helps us to trust in God's promises and to believe that He is with us, even when we cannot see Him. It gives us the courage to stand firm in the face of the enemy's attacks, knowing that God is our shield and protector.

Moreover, faith helps us to resist the devil and his schemes. When the enemy tries to tempt us or discourage us, we can counter his lies with the truth of God's word. By meditating on Scripture and holding fast to its promises, we can gain victory over the enemy's attacks.

In addition, faith helps us to pray effectively. When we pray in faith, we are trusting that God hears our prayers and that He will answer them according to His will. By praying with faith, we can ask for God's protection, guidance, and strength to overcome the enemy's attacks.

Finally, faith helps us to persevere in the midst of trials and hardships. When we face difficult circumstances, we can hold on to the hope that God is with us and that He will bring us through. Our faith gives us the strength to keep pressing on, even when the battle seems long and hard.

In conclusion, faith is a powerful weapon in spiritual warfare. It helps us to trust in God's promises, resist the enemy's attacks, pray effectively, and persevere in the midst of trials. By relying on our faith in God, we can gain victory over the enemy and live a life that is pleasing to Him.

The power of spiritual meditation

Meditating on Scripture is a powerful tool for spiritual warfare. It is a way to renew our minds, fill our hearts with God's truth, and equip us for the battles we face. When we meditate on Scripture, we are not simply reading it, but we are actively engaging with it, allowing it to penetrate our hearts and minds.

One of the key Scriptures that emphasizes the importance of meditating on God's Word is found in Joshua 1:8: "Do not let this Book of the Law depart from your mouth; meditate on it day and night, so that you may be careful to do everything written in it. Then you will be prosperous and successful."

This verse highlights the importance of meditating on God's Word in order to live a life that is pleasing to Him. When we meditate on Scripture, we are filling our minds with truth and wisdom that can guide us in every aspect of our lives.

Another Scripture that emphasizes the power of meditating on Scripture is found in Psalm 1:2-3: "But his delight is in the law of the Lord, and on his law he meditates day and night. He is like a tree planted by streams of water, which yields its fruit in season and whose leaf does not wither. Whatever he does prospers."

This passage compares a person who meditates on God's Word to a tree that is firmly rooted and fruitful. When we meditate on Scripture, we are nourishing our souls and strengthening our faith, which in turn allows us to bear fruit and live a life that brings glory to God.

One of the benefits of meditating on Scripture is that it helps us to combat negative thoughts and emotions. In 2 Corinthians 10:5, Paul writes, "We demolish arguments and every pretension that sets itself up against the knowledge of God, and we take captive every thought to make it obedient to Christ."

When we meditate on God's Word, we are filling our minds with truth that can help us to combat the lies and negative thoughts that the enemy tries to plant in our minds. We can take every thought captive and make it obedient to Christ, which allows us to overcome the enemy's attacks.

Finally, meditating on Scripture helps us to draw closer to God and deepen our relationship with Him. In Psalm 119:15-16, the psalmist writes, "I meditate on your precepts and consider your ways. I delight in your decrees; I will not neglect your word."

When we meditate on God's Word, we are not only gaining wisdom and strength for the battles we face, but we are also delighting in the Lord and growing closer to Him. As we meditate on Scripture, we can experience His presence and His love in a deeper way.

In conclusion, meditating on Scripture is a powerful tool for spiritual warfare. It helps us to renew our minds, combat negative thoughts, draw closer to God, and live a life that is pleasing to Him. Let us make it a daily practice to meditate on God's Word, and allow His truth to transform our hearts and minds.

Practical guide of renewing your mind

Renewing your mind with the Word of God is an essential part of spiritual growth and warfare. It involves intentionally replacing negative thoughts and worldly perspectives with the truth of God's Word. Here are some practical steps you can take to renew your mind with the Word of God:

1. Set aside time for Bible study and meditation. Find a quiet place where you can focus on God's Word without distractions. Set a specific time each day to study and meditate on the Scriptures.

2. Choose a portion of Scripture to focus on. Select a passage of Scripture that speaks to your current situation or challenges. Start by reading it slowly and thoughtfully, taking time to reflect on its meaning.

3. Write down key verses and truths. As you read and study the Scriptures, jot down key verses and truths that stand out to you. Write them on index cards or in a journal where you can refer to them later.

4. Memorize Scripture. Committing verses to memory is an excellent way to renew your mind with the Word of God. Repeat the verses out loud several times, and practice recalling them throughout the day.

5. Pray over the Scriptures. As you meditate on God's Word, ask Him to reveal its truth to you and help you apply it to your life. Pray for wisdom, guidance, and understanding as you seek to renew your mind.

6. Apply the Scriptures to your life. Use the verses and truths you have learned to combat negative thoughts and replace them with God's truth. Choose to believe what God says about you and your situation, even if it

goes against what the world says.

7. Surround yourself with other believers. Spend time with other believers who will encourage and support you in your journey to renew your mind with the Word of God. Attend a Bible study, join a small group, or find a mentor who can guide you along the way.

Remember, renewing your mind with the Word of God is not a one-time event, but a lifelong process. It takes discipline and intentionality, but the rewards are immeasurable. As you commit to renewing your mind with the Word of God, you will find that your thoughts, attitudes, and actions begin to align with His will, and you will experience a greater sense of peace, joy, and purpose in your life.

Spiritual warfare prayer guideline

Here are some points for spiritual warfare prayers for protection, healing, and deliverance from the evil one:

1. **Protection:**

- Pray for God's protection over yourself, your family, and your loved ones.
- Ask God to place a hedge of protection around you and keep you safe from harm.
- Declare that no weapon formed against you shall prosper, and every tongue that rises against you in judgment shall be condemned.
- Claim the promise of Psalm 91 for protection and safety.

1. **Healing:**

- Pray for physical, emotional, and spiritual healing for yourself or someone you know who is in need.
- Ask God to heal any wounds, hurts, or brokenness that may be hindering you or your loved one from experiencing His fullness.
- Declare that by Jesus' stripes, you are healed and made whole.
- Claim the promises of Isaiah 53:5 and James 5:14-15 for healing.

1. **Deliverance:**

- Pray for deliverance from any bondage, addiction, or stronghold that may be holding you or someone you know captive.
- Ask God to break any chains that are binding you or your loved one and set you free.
- Declare that you have been rescued from the domain of darkness and transferred to the kingdom of His beloved Son.
- Claim the promises of Psalm 107:14 and Galatians 5:1 for freedom and deliverance.

Remember, spiritual warfare prayers are not about manipulating God or trying to control Him, but rather about submitting to His will and aligning our hearts and minds with His. As you pray for protection, healing, and deliverance, seek His guidance and trust in His perfect timing and plan for your life.

Don't miss out!

Visit the website below and you can sign up to receive emails whenever Johannes Tefo publishes a new book. There's no charge and no obligation.

https://books2read.com/r/B-A-UEZX-EXUGC

BOOKS2READ

Connecting independent readers to independent writers.

Did you love *Deliver Your Soul From Evil*? Then you should read *Identity In Christ*[1] by Johannes Tefo!

IDENTITY IN CHRIST

JOHANNES TEFO

2

Uncover who you truly are in Christ with "Identity in Christ"! This book helps you see yourself differently, with stories and easy-to-understand lessons. It's like a guide showing you how loved and special you are to God. You'll learn to be confident and find your purpose, feeling free from doubts and fears. If you're unsure about yourself or want to feel closer to God, this book is for you. Get ready to be inspired and discover the awesome person you were meant to be. Dive into "Identity in Christ" now and start your journey to feeling whole and loved!

1. https://books2read.com/u/bzry0L

2. https://books2read.com/u/bzry0L

Also by Johannes Tefo

Family spiritual Warfare Books
Youth's Guide To Spiritual Warfare
A Women's Guide To Spiritual Warfare

Standalone
Deliver Your Soul From Evil
Overcoming Spirit Of Stagnation
The 24: Prophetic Word For This Season 2024 And Beyond
Michael For Warfare
Territorial Spirits: Overcome Evil Strongholds in Your Life And
Take Over Your Community With Strategic Warfare And Winning Prayers
Prayers Against Suicide Spirit
Spiritual Warfare When Enough is Enough
Identity In Christ
Prayers Against Satanic Networks
The Workplace You Need: Spiritual Warfare Prayers That Silence Evil Powers At Your Workplace.

About the Author

Before he started writing Christian books, Johannes got a graduate degree in Film and Television from university of Johannesburg. After that, just to shake things up, he went to equip himself with religious studies, particularly Christianity, just to have knack about the world beyond the curtains of time. And how this body of Christ has transformed millions of people around the world, not neglecting how sadly the movement has been persecuted from time to time. He now writes full time.